Fragments Of A Fading Testimony

Deconstructing My Mormon Faith Through Poetry

Maddi Lee

BookLeaf Publishing

India | USA | UK

Made with ❤ on the BookLeaf Publishing Platform
www.bookleafpub.in
www.bookleafpub.com

Dedication

To all those who are struggling with their faith--you are not alone.

Preface

I was born as a member of the Church of Jesus Christ of Latter-Day Saints, a Christian religion whose headquarters are based in the state of Utah. I was born in Utah County, where most of my classmates were also LDS and it was just assumed that everyone lived the religion.

The religion itself is a very high-demand religion. They have "commandments" that direct your life every single step of the way. I was taught how to worship, how to dress, what I should and shouldn't eat, how I should speak, what I should and shouldn't do on Sundays, and how much money I should give the church.

Then, when I was older, I was taught to serve a mission, to preach the gospel to other "less fortunate" people. It was implied that I was better than other people who were not LDS because I was part of God's chosen people. And that it was my job as part of the "chosen ones" to share the goodness with others by preaching baptism to them, so that they might also be "saved."

After returning home from a mission, I was taught to marry as soon as possible, have kids as soon as possible, and have as many kids as possible. I was even taught how to raise those kids to be good disciples of Christ, just how I was raised.

Being LDS was relatively easy. They tell you what to do in every step of your life, so that you don't have to think or worry about what you're going to do. You know that, if you do all these things, you will have a good, blessed life, and the promise of eternal life with your family when you die. Because they tell you how to live every part of your life, you never have to once think for yourself if you don't want to.

And that was the happy little bubble that I lived in for 25 years of my life. 25 years of following commands with no questions asked, of doing everything "the right way" without even considering that their way might not be the only right way. 25 years of being told that I was better than other people, because I was born into this religion and they weren't, and actually believing it.

Not everything sat right with me though. There were times where my soul was in conflict with the teachings that I was being taught, where things being said just didn't feel right with my soul. I noticed the conflict, but I didn't notice that I was feeling inner conflict. I thought those feelings were influences of Satan, since we are taught that if we sin, we take ourselves further away from God, and make ourselves more susceptible to the impressions of the adversary.

But those feelings were there, and they kept growing, little by little over the years. Then at 25, I became a mom. I was still going to college, despite having become a mother, and in college I was being exposed to new ways of thinking. I was taking culture classes, that taught me about hard subjects like gender, critical race theory, critical thinking skills, and I was learning about different cultures and societies.

These things I was learning in college, paired with me being the new caretaker of a tiny human, slowly changed the ways I thought and felt, and my beliefs started shifting. Instead of doing things without asking, I wanted to know why I was doing them. Instead of believing there was only one right way to live life, I started seeing that other ways of living might also be right. Instead of reacting without thinking, I wanted to actively think for myself.

This shift in my thought process triggered the most difficult part of my life--I started going through a faith crisis. My inside world was shattering and I didn't know what to do. I was afraid to reach out to anyone because if

I did, it would mean acknowledging that there was
something wrong with my life. So I lived alone with
these thoughts for a year or two, not knowing what to
do.

So that's when I started to process my thoughts and
feelings through poetry. In school, I always loved taking
classes that brought out creativity in some way. I don't
consider myself to be an excellent writer, but I still took
a creative writing class, because the idea of being
creative with words was always intriguing to me. I liked
the poetry assignments because it was a short style of
writing that you could express a lot of emotions with. So
I decided that I would use my creative writing class to
process the thoughts and feelings of my faith crisis.

So I wrote some poems for the class, and I kept writing
poems even after the class ended. And that's how I
processed my faith crisis until I was ready to talk about
it with others. I've decided to put these poems in a book
because going through a faith crisis without telling
anyone was really lonely. And I am hoping that, by
sharing my poems with the world, someone else out
there might not feel as lonely as I did.

Acknowledgements

There are several people who have been a big part of my journey. Without these people influencing my life, I would not be where I am today. These people are my heroes:

My dad, Tracey: He was the first in our immediate family to leave the church. He made it easier for me to leave when I was ready.

My best friend, Kyrie: Without her love and support, I would probably be even more of a hot mess than I currently am.

My daughter, Rayla: Without becoming her mom, I may have never considered why I blindly followed the leaders of the church without asking questions. Without seeing her strong and willful personality, I may have never wanted that same personality for myself.

My favorite author, Brandon Sanderson: His fantasy and science fiction novels have lots of religious and cultural themes from different ways of believing and living. Through the stories in his books, I have been exposed to a lot of different belief systems and ways of thinking.

The characters and events may be fictional, but the themes and perspectives are not. And I am grateful to be able to empathize with those perspectives.

My mission president: When my mission service was over, I told him I was afraid to get married, because that's what's supposed to be on the mind of every returned missionary. He told me that it's okay if I don't want to be married, but to allow myself the permission to change my mind if I ever think differently. I know he probably never thought that I would use that advice in the middle of a faith crisis, but the idea that I can give myself permission to change my mind if I think differently has been a recurring theme as I have transitioned away from religion. His advice helped me to give myself the permission to leave.

Everyone else: There are so many people I have met in my life, who have helped me become who I am today. These people are friends, family, and acquaintances. I am grateful for how I have been shaped by everyone in my life.

1. Perfect

I don't want to be
Perfect--I just want to be
Good enough for me.

2. No God

No god dictates the
Paths that I choose for my life.
Each choice is my own.

3. All In

I was all in,
Until I wasn't.

I checked all the boxes,
Until I stopped checking them.

I did everything I was supposed to do,
Until I didn't.

I didn't think I would ever change,
Until I did.

I thought I knew everything I needed to know,
Now I know I still have lots to learn.

And knowing what I know now,
There's no way I can go back.

4. Check The Boxes

[x] Be born in the covenant to an earthly father and mother
[x] Receive a baby blessing
[x] Go to Primary and learn about becoming perfect through Christ
[x] Get baptized
[x] Receive the gift of the Holy Ghost
[x] Take the sacrament for the first time
[x] Take the sacrament weekly for the rest of your life
[ ] Receive the Aaronic priesthood (only applies to boys)
[ ] Pass the sacrament as a deacon (only applies to boys)
[ ] Go to Young Mens (only applies to boys)
[x] Go to Young Womens (only applies to girls)
[x] Get a limited-use temple recommend
[x] Do baptisms for the dead in the temple
[ ] Bless the sacrament as a teacher/priest (only applies to boys who have the Aaronic priesthood)
[x] Receive your Young Women's Medallion (only applies to girls)
[ ] Complete your Eagle Scout (only applies to boys)
[x] Go to Seminary
[x] Receive your patriarchal blessing
[x] Graduate from seminary
[x] Apply to serve a mission and receive a mission call

[x] Receive your endowment at the temple

[ ] Receive the Melchizedek priesthood at the temple
(only applies to boys who have the Aaronic priesthood)

[x] Return to the temple to complete saving ordinances
for the dead

[x] Serve an honorable mission (18 months for girls, 24
months for boys)

[x] Go to the singles' ward

[x] Become a temple ordinance worker

[x] Find an eternal companion

[x] Marry in the temple for time and all eternity

[x] Fulfill your duties as a minister to those you are
called to minister to

[x] Say yes to serving in whatever calling you are asked
to do

[x] Have a child

[ ] Have as many children, as soon as possible, and as
close together as possible

[ ] Raise your children in the church

[ ] Continue to minister and say yes to all the callings
you are asked to serve in

[ ] Happily stay married for time and all eternity

[ ] Endure to the end of this life so you can have eternal
happiness in the next life

5. Regrets of a 17 Year Old Girl

My experiences are mine,
But I am not my experiences.

At least that's what I tell myself.

It's hard to convince yourself
Of something you don't
Fully
Believe.

I was careful,
I was cautious
To the point of paranoia.
My defenses were strong.
I let no one in.

No one until you that is.

You were gentle,
You were kind.
You were harmless as a fly.

But you weren't the fly.

I was.
You were the spider.

You were handsome,
Even charming!
You had quite the way with girls.
Your beauty eased my worries
Until I dropped my defenses
Completely.

And then you spun your webs.

I didn't know I was trapped,
I thought my shields were up!
Your attacks were thoughtfully disguized
As ideas that were mine,
Not yours.

First, you pushed verbally,
I pushed back.
Then you got physical,
I pushed back.

Then you pushed *harder.*

And I collapsed.

I was stuck in your web
That I didn't even know you were spinning
And it was too strong to escape.

Or maybe
I was too weak to escape.

How long was I trapped,
Thinking it was my fault?

You said I put
Unwanted
Thoughts
In your mind.
And *I* felt guilty.
The guilt was your venom
Slowly breaking me
Day by day.

You said you would leave *me*
If I didn't comply
With your requests,
You said no one else
Would want me
After what we'd done.
So I stayed
Too afraid

And unable to escape.

You said I played an equal part
Because I didn't say no.
It's true.
I didn't say no.
But I also never said yes.

Was I *actually* guilty?
Did I consent by *accident*?
Am I trying to justify sin?

Why am I
Still wondering
A decade later
If it actually counts
As sexual assault?

It does, by the way.
I looked it up.

Even so,
It's hard to believe
That I was deceived,
Trapped,
And consumed
By a predator.

My experiences are mine
But I am *not* my experiences.
At least that's what I tell myself
Again and again
And again.

Maybe
Someday
I'll actually believe it.

6. Can Families Really Be Together Forever?

The unofficial second verse to the LDS hymn, Families Can Be Together Forever

I have a family here on earth.
It's broken and messy.
Parents aren't married
and they've lost their faith entirely.

Families can be together forever,
But it's not guaranteed.
It's all conditional and everyone must be
Living perfectly or they won't be
Together for eternity.

7. Ordinances

Baptism
In the house of god.
A watery rebirth
From darkness into light.
A way to show
Your devotion to Jesus.
But why baptize a child
Only at the age of eight?
Shouldn't a lifelong commitment
Be decided by an adult?

Confirmation
After baptism
To seal the deal.
Hands on head,
Hair still wet,
A Holy Spirit Is given
To be your lifelong guide
Through life.
But why must we
Be scrubbed of sin
Before given a guardian angel?
Are we not worthy of help
Before then?

Initiatory

In the temple of god.
A house of white,
No dirt in sight.
Cleanliness that resembles
The state of the heavens.
Initiation into a higher way
Of serving god.
An expanse on
Your baptismal covenant.
Anointing with oil,
Washing with water.
"Your sins are forgiven,
"You are clean every whit."
But why are my sins
Forgiven twice now?
Wasn't that covered
In baptism?
Why is a second forgiveness required,
If the first was supposedly sufficient?

Endowment

After initiatory
To prepare you for a higher way of living.
Now you are clean
So you can progress further.

A new name given
For a new start to life.
"Your new name is
Eliza."
Pledged to God and joyful.
A fitting name
For a "second baptism."

In the endowment room,
Men on one side,
Women on the other.
Why is there segregation
In the house of God?
"Anyone who does not wish to proceed,
Please leave now"
What's going to happen next,
If they're giving me a chance to abort?
"Elohim created the world with Jehova,
Together they created animals and man."
Why are two men creating life on earth?
I thought male and female
Produced life together.

Covenants made,
Sealed with signs and tokens.
Why am I being asked to make these promises
For a second time?

I thought this was all covered
By my baptism.
"Covenant to heed
To the counsel of your husband."
Why do I need a man
In order to commune with god?
Has God not heard any
Of my prayers thus far?
Satan comes to warn
"Keep your covenants or else."
Why is Satan in the temple,
If this is the house of God?

Circle in prayer,
"Women veil your faces."
Am I not good enough
To be in the presence of god?
At the veil, new name is given,
And tokens repeated.
Why do I need a code
To get into heaven?
Wouldn't god know
I just covenanted with him?
In the celestial room,
My parents are waiting for me.
Will this be what
Heaven feels like?

An eternity of repeating
promises and passwords,
For silent reassurance
Of my worth?

Sealing

After endowment,
The eternal way of marriage.
Not just for time,
But for eternity too.
The last covenant needed
To make it to heaven.
Why can't I be saved in heaven
Without a spouse?
"Tell your husband
Your new name at the veil."
Is my husband
Representing god?

Covenant to spouse
To combine your lives into one.
To love each other in sickness and health,
In poor and wealth.
But what about loving each other
in religious differences?
Friends and family
Come to congratulate.

"You did it!"
"You finally made it!"
Why are they praising me
For making it to marriage?
So much more in life
Happens after the union.

Endure to the end
What does that even mean?
Repetition,

Renewal,

Repentance,

Until the end of days.

When your body joins the earth

And your soul moves on,

With a promise

That if you were faithful in this life,

You can have glory in the next.

But how do you know if you were faithful enough?

Most never find out.

Second Anointing
Reserved for some,

But not all.

The spiritual version

Of lather, rinse, repeat.

A confirmation

That your spot in heaven
Is guaranteed,
That your efforts in this life
Took you to the Celestial Kingdom.
"But shhhh!
Don't tell!
Never tell another soul,
Unless they've also received it."
But how do you know if they've received it?
And why can't this be something
That everyone gets to do?
Are spots in the heavens
Really that scarce?
Perhaps the heavens
Aren't truly
Made for me.

8. A Mother's Prayer

Dear god, why won't my toddler sleep?
Every night I want to weep.

The nights with her are very long,
Please tell me what I'm doing wrong!

I really want to be a good mom,
But at night I'm a ticking bomb!

I feel like it's only a matter of days
Before I explode in regrettable ways.

Please god, I don't want to lose my head!
Please help my toddler go to bed!

9. Don't

Don't tell me how to
Raise the individual
That came from my womb.

10. Dear God

Dear God
I need to apologize
I've been worshipping the wrong deity
My entire life.
This god has taught me lies
Disguised
As love From heavenly eyes
And it's this god I'm growing to despise.

I've been told that
Guilt, shame, and fear
Are characteristics of love
Even though to a child that's damaging
And as a parent,
Loving that way feels absurd.

I've been taught to cleave to my spouse;
That He's the messenger of God for the house.
And I'm nothing without him and children.

God has implied
For Man to cleave to a wife.
And be sure to keep her in line all of life.
Because god gives men the final say.

We learn that Families can be forever
But only If we follow rigorous rules.
And disown the daughters
And shun the sons
Who can't conform.

Because what might happen in death
Is more important
than what's currently happening in life.

God has made it clear he's a man
Who created the world with other men
Even though females have been given
The ability to create
And sustain
Life with their bodies.

God says, "Feel free to question!
Questions are godly and good!
But if you decide
That for you I'm not right,
Then you need to review and repent."

God shouts, "You can leave if you want to!
Follow your heart and then,
While you're paving your own path,

I'll turn everyone against you."

In my life I've seen others leave.
They're the topic of hushed conversation.
(Or not so hushed live-streamed sermons.)
They're the "examples not to follow."

But inside my thoughts,
I can't help but be awed
And silently applaude
Their courage and strength
To challenge this god.

Sometimes I feel like I'm bleeding
from every pore of my soul,
Begging my Heavenly Father for relief
While he sees the pain and suffering
As paternal love.

And amidst the constant struggling
I feel you
Picking my broken body up off the ground
And holding me until my wounds heal.

I hear you telling me it's okay
To be strong,
And leave the life I've known so long,

So I can be the woman I need to be
For both me
And my daughter

I want to heed your call
But every time I fall
Torn by tradition,
Pierced by patriarchy,
And crushing beneath Christianity.

I'm sorry God,
Goddess?
Eternal Being?

I'm scared.
I don't feel prepared
To do what needs to be done.
I fear the strength I have
Isn't strong enough to break free.

So, dear God,
Please forgive me

Sincerely, your lost child

11. Love Unconditionally

Love unconditionally
Even the killer, abuser, and rapist
Even if they're family
Even if they've hurt you
Continue to love and forgive
Even if it means ignoring your personal boundaries

You are children of god
You have infinite potential
But you are also nothing
Too weak to do anything
without god guiding you

Families can be forever
If you live the life of a perfectionist
And judge everyone beneath your high standards

Put your family above all else
Except for god
And shun them if they are gay
Or believe in a different god
Or if god tells you to

Never stop telling others how wrong they are
For having questions
And choosing new beliefs
Even if they've prayed about it
And have received that answer for themselves

Feel free to question!
Questions are good!
But we won't accept all answers.
In fact, you'll only get these answers.
And if you don't,
You obviously did something wrong.

You can leave if you want to
Just know that everyone
And I mean everyone
Will know you're a bad person for doing so.

12. The Natural Man: An Enemy to God?

Inspired by the Mormon Scripture, Mosiah 3:19

Dear god,

If my natural self is your sworn enemy, then how much power do you actually have? How much power does my true self hold, for you to dedicate your immortal ass to hiding that part of myself from me? If you really were all-powerful, my purest self wouldn't need to be your enemy, right?

Wouldn't it make more sense if you wanted me to love myself and reach my full potential, instead of wanting me to run in fear from it? In reality, you must be so weak and insecure in yourself, that the only way you can have power is to make me, and other women like me, feel weak and insecure too.

As an earthly mother, I am appalled that you would call yourself my Heavenly Father. You are nothing like the type of parent I want to be. And I plan to dedicate the rest of my mortal life to making sure my daughter never believes your lies like I did.

Sincerely,

A raging goddess

13. God Must be a Mother

God is the
Creator of Souls

Mothers are the
Creators of bodies

God is the
Nurturer of Spirits

Mothers feed
The spirit's vessel

God is the
Educator of Morals

Mothers develop
A child's character

God is the
Teller of Parables

Mothers are
Readers of bedtime stories

God is the
Oracle of Obedience

Mothers set
Boundaries in the house

God is the
Dealer of Consequences

Mothers teach
Actions have reactions

God is the
Spiritual Comforter

Mothers physically
Comfort their children

All signs point to yes,
God must be a mother.

14. Thank You Satan

Pre-mortal life:
An eternity of spirits
Spiritually stuck
Unable to progress
Until Lucifer suggested a new plan
Which brings us to,

Earth life:
Adam and Eve
First people of earth
Eternally stuck
In the garden of Eden
Until the serpent
Gave Eve
The fruit of knowledge
And the ability to think for herself.
Which transitions to,

Life after Eden:
People can procreate,
Have posterity,
Teach morals,
Choose their core beliefs,
Think for themselves,

Learn new things,
Invent new creations,
Inspire generations,
And never stop progressing.

All thanks to Satan

15. Pieces

We got high on each other.
It was my first time,
I felt like my life was shattered.
My picture-perfect existence
Had broken into a thousand pieces.
You were there with me
To mourn what I thought would be.

We built a puzzle
Under the influence of Christianity.
It wasn't easy,
But it was easier than facing
My current plight.
I cried and vented, you held me tight.
I wanted that moment to last forever.

I thought you were the missing piece
To my broken puzzle.
Life felt complete with you in it.
I felt like I could face my challenges
Because you were by my side.
Because you empowered me,
I felt like I could do anything.

But you weren't the missing piece.
You weren't the finishing touch.
Our lives went in opposite directions.
Our time together was gone in a flash.
And all I am left with are memories.
But you're still a piece of my shattered life.
And I'm picking up the pieces again.

16. No Longer Compatible

I thought I was the lid to your pot.
You thought you were the lid to mine.
We fit fairly well together,
Complementary most of the time.

But our pots were not the same size,
Our lids were not the same shape.
We didn't notice the difference,
Until it was too late.

The focus wasn't on the shape,
Nor was it on the size.
The goal was to make us fit,
So we could join our lives.

So there we started our lives,
Not quite a perfect fit.
We teetered on the edge,
Trying hard not to slip.

We danced this dance for years,
Thinking we were fine.
Then things became more tricky,
And harder to walk the line.

We started looking closer,
At the lids and pots.
Realizing they weren't the same at all,
There were differences–there were lots.

Now we sat with those differences,
Not knowing what to do.
Should we split to find better matches?
Should we stick together and push through?

For months we weighed our options,
Should we stay, or should we go?
Neither were sounding great,
And no easy way to know.

We tried to make things work,
We gave each other a chance.
But things now felt awkward,
Our new knowledge changed the dance.

We couldn't go on like this,
It wasn't any way to live.
We just weren't compatible,
We had no more to give.

I'm sorry that I wasn't
The one you were looking for.
I'm sorry I ended up being
More of a difficult chore.

But now our lives are split,
We are not one, but two.
I hope you can find your someone,
Your better half that's true.

I loved and learned a lot from you,
From our time together.
And while saying goodbye hurts,
I hope our futures are better.

17. To Whom It May Concern

Our lives are on opposite paths,
We travel quickly in different directions.
In careers,
In religious beliefs,
In sexual preferences.
We are two cakes
Made from different molds,
Our experiences being the ingredients
That give us our unique flavors.

I used to think we were slices from the same cake.
We were raised in similar ways,
We believed in the same things,
And even shared like experiences.
But I mistook the frosting for the cake itself.
Frosting that you've now scraped off,
Letting your inner layers and flavors show.

Your flavors are strong,
Your layers are many.
Some think it's overpowering.
But you don't let that stop you.
You keep sharing your flavors with the world,

You say frosting-less cake is the way to go.
The only way to truly live your life.

I'm happy for you, truly.
I'm glad you have the confidence to say what you say,
And feel what you feel.
But I'm also afraid.

I'm afraid because my flavors
Are different from yours.
And if I shed my frosting,
You will know.
You will know we have different beliefs,
Different hopes and dreams.
You will see that we aren't as similar as
We may seem.

You've rejected ingredients
That I still cherish.
Some days I wonder if I should
Reject them too,
But I haven't.
Because I've been told they will enhance my quality,
And I still hope that's true.

I love being your friend.
I'm grateful that our paths have crossed.

But they say you should be careful who you hate,
Because it could be someone you love.
And I feel like I am the person you hate,
Because of what I've chosen to love,
And you just haven't noticed yet.

I feel like I will eventually scrape my frosting off.
So when that day comes for me,
And you see my hidden flavors,
I just hope we can still be friends.

18. My Own Pioneer

There are six generations of pioneers
That paved the way before me.
Six long generations
That go back to Nauvoo,
Who listened to Joseph Smith,
And believed his every word.

Six dedicated generations
That followed Brigham Young to Utah,
A land of empty soil,
Far away from outside influence,
Where church leaders could plant
Their ideas and codes of conduct
Into docile young minds.

Six uneducated generations
Of following commandments
Without asking questions,
Of believing one man's story
As factual nonfiction.

Six docile generations
Who never stepped outside of the box
Because they were told they were free

And the rest of the world
Were the real prisoners.

Six generations,
But not six more.
Because this way of thinking,
It ends with me.
I will think for myself.
I will question.
I will put theories to the test.
I will study and research.
I will contradict ludicrous claims.
I will raise my children to think for themselves.
I will pave new paths.
I will inspire future generations.
I will be
My own pioneer.

19. Staying or Straying

A reversible poem: read the lines top to bottom first, then read them bottom to top.

I have to leave.

Nothing makes me think

Staying is a good idea.

That's why I think

People who see differently often leave.

Because

Deep-rooted culture is slow to divergence.

Which is why

This is a challenge.

But I know

I want to be the change.

I think;

I ponder what I can do.

So,

I choose to leave.

I can't make a difference if

I stay in.

20. Last One

It's easy to walk a path
When many before you
Have padded down the way.

But what do you do
When everyone has left the path
And the way is covered in weeds,
Making it hard to see where to go?

It's easy to row upstream
When you are canoeing with a friend
Who is there to help you row.

But what do you do
When your friend decides to bail
And jumps out of the boat,
Leaving you to struggle alone?

It's easy to swim out to sea
When the waves are calm
and the tide is low.

But what do you do
When a storm hits

And waves crash over you,
Threatening to make you drown?

It's easy to fight zombies
When you have a team of zombie slayers
And a full arsenal.

But what do you do
When one by one
Zombies pick off your friends
And you're fighting alone?

It's easy to believe in God
When your whole family does too
And nobody questions his existence.

But what do you do
when your family stops believing
And rejects religion completely,
Saying their life is better for it?

What do you do
When your path is unclear?

What do you do
When you've lost strength to row?

What do you do
When you're drowning in waves?

What do you do
When you're the last man standing?

What do you do
When you're the last believer hoping?

And how in the hell
Do you find the strength to do it?

21. 85 Steps to Losing Your Faith

1: Be born into the Church of Jesus Christ of Latter-Day Saints. Notice all growing up how church members treat boys and girls differently because boys can have the priesthood but girls cannot. Notice that God's "unconditional love" comes with conditions.

2: Be told that you have divine potential, but that you are nothing and can be nothing without Jesus, and *actually believe it.* Be told that you are perfect and cannot sin until you turn 8 years old. Be afraid of how your time as a perfect being on earth has an expiration date.

3: Get baptized at 8 and be told that you're perfect still, but that if you sin, you will not get to go to heaven with your family. Strive to be perfect in everything you do to stay perfect enough for heaven. Have a severe meltdown when your mom tells you that the spoiled apple juice you drank was actually wine, because it means that you've broken the word of wisdom and are now imperfect.

4: Be invited by non-member friends to birthday parties that take place on Sundays. Be told by your mom that

you can't go to those birthday parties because they are
being held on Sundays, and that going to a birthday
party on a Sunday is not keeping the Sabbath day holy.
Be told to tell your friends, to their face, that you can't
attend their party because it is against your religious
beliefs. Have your mom tell you that this is an
opportunity to be a missionary for your church. Instead,
feel sad that you can't go, and feel like you are telling
your friend that you are "too good" to go to their party.

5: Turn 12 and continue to notice the sexism within the
patriarchal lds church. Be told that it's your job as a
young woman to keep the minds of boys morally clean
by masking your body with as much fabric as possible.
Be sexually assaulted by your boyfriend at 17, then be
told that you had sinned and need to repent for your
mistakes.

6: Confess to your bishop that you let your boyfriend
have his way with you and be told that you are forgiven.
Feel unworthy of living and unloved by God despite
having confessed to your bishop and repented. Strive to
be perfect in all things to make up for how badly you
sinned, so that you might someday be forgiven and
accepted into heaven still.

7: Hear the October 2012 announcement that boys can

now serve missions at 18 and girls can serve at 19. Feel the desire to serve a mission but worry that your worthiness will keep you from doing so. Pray about serving a mission and decide that it's what you want to do.

8: Apply to serve a mission but be told by church headquarters that your social anxiety is too high to actually serve a mission. Secretly worry that the real reason might be because you were never actually forgiven for your teenage transgressions. Spend a year going out with the local missionaries, teaching lessons in relief society, and giving talks in sacrament meeting to prove to headquarters that you are, in fact, worthy and capable of serving a mission.

9: Receive a patriarchal blessing and be told that you are destined for missionary work and to be a leader in the church. Also be told that you are destined to be a wife and mother. Wonder why you haven't been called on a mission yet if your patriarchal blessings says you will be given the opportunity to do so.

10: Finally be called to serve in the Florida Tallahassee Mission! Make preparations to go to the temple. Purchase your temple garments but be told that you are not allowed to wear them until after you receive your endowment. Worry about the fabric options and the fit of the underwear when you won't even be able to try them on for size.

11: Go to the temple to receive your endowment. Be told in Initiatory that your sins are forgive and you are clean again. Wonder why they are saying that if baptism was supposed to be what washed your sins away. Wonder if this is some sort of "second baptism" and be hopeful that your sexual sins of high school are now truly forgiven.

12: Receive your new name in the temple and proceed to the endowment room. Hear the officiator give anyone present a "chance to leave" before the ceremony starts. Panic and wonder if you should leave, but also stay put because you have to receive your endowment in order to serve the mission you've been working so hard to serve.

13: Go through your first endowment session in the temple and come out concerned that you've promised to always heed to the counsel of your husband, not God, when you aren't even getting married. Wonder how you should heed to the counsel of God on your mission if you don't yet have a husband. Realize that you don't want to put your life solely in the hands of your husband, and become afraid of ever getting married.

14: Attend the temple for the second time with your family. Notice that life on earth is created by God and Jesus. Wonder why two men created life in the temple, when man and woman create life together on earth.

15: Arrive at the Missionary Training Center three weeks before Christmas. Question your worthiness to serve a mission and have a mental breakdown in the MTC. Be reassured by your branch president of your worthiness and leave for the mission field.

16: Arrive in your mission area and receive your first companion. Notice that there are only white people in your ward, and you are in the deep south where you know the population has more diversity than that.

17: Have fights constantly with your companion because approaching random people on the streets to talk about Jesus doesn't feel right to you and it's sending you into anxiety attacks weekly. At the end of the transfer, request a different companion and have your mission president chastise you for requesting a different companion.

18: Be given two new, very patient and understanding companions, and finish your training in a trio. Be hopeful that being a missionary can be fun and enjoyable too. Be sad when your time in this trio comes to an end.

19: Be given the companion from Hell who continually reminds you that you are not a good missionary because street contacting is hard for you, and often tells you that you are going to go to Hell for not reaching out to more people. Have your first full-blown panic attack and suffer from suicidal ideation from serving with this companion.

20: Meet with a therapist and be suggested by the therapist to take medication for anxiety and depression. Be afraid to take medication because of the implications, deny it, then decide later to try it, only to be told that you missed your chance when you had it and be denied medication the second time.

21: Spend a year with your favorite companion, who also happens to be your most free-spirited companion. Baptize two children of a nonmember single mother, who doesn't want to be baptized. Wonder if you did a good thing by baptizing the kids, or if you did a bad thing because that family cannot be together forever if the mom doesn't convert.

22: Confess to your mission president your sexual sins with your boyfriend in high school on four separate occasions, each time being reassured by him that you're fine because you already confessed to your bishop. Still have doubts about your worthiness as a misisonary.

23: Hear about other sister missionaries becoming leaders and training new missionaries and dream about the day when you will be called to either train or serve as a leader. Hope that this day will come.

24: Go to missionary conferences throughout your mission and hear your mission president constantly preach about how the most important decisions you will ever make in life will be who you marry, where you marry, and when you marry, and have your fear of marriage rekindled.

25: Learn that gay marriage is legalized throughout the country and have it become a heavy topic of discussion for you and the other missionaries. Hear about the 2015 announcement that bans children of LGBTQ couples from being baptized, realize that half the ward is leaving because of it, and feel the first hint of anger towards the church bubble within you. Pray and reconcile this anger by convincing yourself that the reason why god doesn't want to baptize kids of LGBTQ families is because he doesn't want to eternally break up their families.

26: Move to a new area and have the success of baptizing a convert, but deny another investigator baptism for having gone to jail multiple times. Feel heartbroken that your investigator cannot be baptized despite having a converted heart.

27: Receive your second companion from Hell during the last three months of your mission, have more panic attacks, and suffer from suicidal ideation again. Pray daily that God will create some disaster for you that will send you back to heaven.

28: Come to the end of your mission and never get called to be a leader or a trainer. Lose faith in the promises written in your patriarchal blessing.

29: Confess to your mission president before going home that you are afraid to get married, and have your mission president respond by asking you if you are gay (because that must be the only reason why a young woman wouldn't want to get married). Have your mission president tell you that it's okay that you don't want to get married now, but allow yourself the permission to change your mind if the right guy comes along.

30: Return home and tell all your friends and family about how great your mission was because that's what you're supposed to do. (And omitting the hard parts isn't necessarily lying.)

31: Return to the temple for the first time since leaving for your mission. Go through an endowment session and realize that the creation story being told depicts two men creating life on earth together, when you've been taught all your life that men and women co-create life. Feel frustrated by the fact that women have to veil their faces during the prayer ceremony. Wonder why women can't show their faces when communing with God in the temple but men can.

32: Try going to the singles' ward, to brave your fear of dating and marriage, and feel darkness the minute you step into the building. Get anxious and leave. Never go back to the singles' ward. Never ask guys out on dates, because that would bring you closer to marriage.

33: Get a job selling temple clothing at Deseret Book, and be told that you can't tell people to modify their garments in any way at all, and get in trouble when you sell petite bottoms to a 6-foot tall girl.

34: Say goodbye to your sister who is going to serve a mission in Seattle. Wish her the best and hope that her mission experience won't be as traumatic as yours.

35: Have your parents tell you that they are separating
and likely getting a divorce. Question why your parents
are getting a divorce when God is supposed to bless your
family because you served a mission. Wonder if you
didn't serve your mission worthily enough for your
family to receive blessings.

36: Go on a date with a friend from high school 4 months
after your mission because you haven't been on a date
since before serving a mission and you feel ready to take
your mission president's advice about allowing yourself
to change your mind if the opportunity presents itself. A
month later start dating and calling each other boyfriend
and girlfriend.

37: Become a temple ordinance worker and start working
at the temple with your boyfriend. learn during your
shifts working at the temple that "temple names" are
rotated through on a monthly basis, so your temple
name isn't as special as you originally thought it to be.

38: Have your boyfriend tell you three months later that
he prayed about you two getting married and he feels
like it's the right thing for you two to do. Pray about
what your boyfriend has said and decide that marrying
him feels okay (it's also the next step in mormon

culture).

39: Tell your families that you are wanting to get
married, take engagement photos, and book a wedding
date all before officially getting engaged. Officially get
engaged three months later and get married the same
year that your parents' divorce is finalized.

40: On your wedding day, tell your husband your temple
name at the veil and find out that you don't get to know
his temple name in return. Wonder why he gets to
represent God and know your secret name when you
don't get to know his in return. Get married in the
temple without your dad and best friend present,
because they are not worthy to enter the temple. Later
regret your choice to be married in the temple for that
reason.

41: Struggle to have sex with your husband because you
still feel guilty about what you did in high school. Have a
rough honeymoon because of it.

42: Eagerly move into your first apartment with your
new husband, join a new ward, and eagerly accept your
calling as a nursery teacher. Joyously participate in your
church calling and ministering duties, and not so
joyously participate in your sexual duties as a wife.

43: Watch your dad get remarried outside of the temple. Grieve the loss of your eternal family. Worry about what will happen to your family in the next life.

44: Get in trouble for wanting to do a Halloween craft with your nursery kids because it's not "in the handbook." Get released from your calling, without anyone telling you why, and corner your bishop after church to ask him "why the hell" you got released without being told.

45: Now that you're released from nursery, go to relief society and Sunday school. Notice that men and women in the church are treated just as differently as the boys and girls are treated. Feel frustrated by those differences and start growing angry towards patriarchy. Find any excuse you can to not go to relief society.

46: Hear the 2019 announcement that church will now be 2 hours instead of 3 and that relief society will be held every other Sunday. Call the weeks of relief society "Segregation Sunday" because men and women are separated. Struggle attending church on those weeks.

47: Have your husband bring up the topic of children, because you've been married for almost two years and his parents had him on their second anniversary. Tell your husband that you want to finish school before having kids, and have that be the end of the conversation.

48: Get the urge to be a mother a few months later, tell your husband, and have your husband laugh as if you just told a hilarious joke. Hear that your sister-in-law is pregnant and burst into tears because you want to be a mom too.

49: Spend hours sobbing and praying to god to heal your heart and change your husband's mind about having a kid. When those prayers aren't answered, angrily pray for something bad to happen to your sister-in-law. Later pray for forgiveness for acting in jealousy.

50: Rejoice when your sister comes home from her mission, bond over similar mission stories, and be slightly jealous that she got to be a trainer and a leader on her mission. Wonder if God won't let you be a mother because you were never a leader or trainer on your mission. After all, your experiences on your mission are supposed to foreshadow your experiences in the rest of your life.

51: Listen to your dad tell you that he and his wife are

leaving the church. Wonder why this is happening when your family is supposed to be blessed for your sacrifice of serving a mission. Wonder what you did wrong as a missionary to have this happen to your family. Wonder what will happen now that your dad is no longer sealed to you in the next life.

52: Convince your husband you are serious about having a child and take the steps necessary to get pregnant. Get pregnant on your second wedding anniversary and tell all your friends and family about it. Have your family celebrate the good news with you.

53: Throw up every day while pregnant, pray for god to take your sickness away, and have him never answer your prayers. Hate being pregnant and wonder if you will be a terrible mother because of it.

54: Learn that women can now be witnesses to saving ordinances like baptism and marriage, when they couldn't previously. Have your sister ask you to be a witness at her wedding. Graciously accept and watch your sister get married in the temple without your mom or dad present. Feel happy for your sister that she gets to be married, but feel sad that your parents couldn't participate. Feel frustrated that the church won't even let non members be present for a marriage.

55: Realize that you don't want your parents and siblings left out of major life events even if they aren't members of the church. Realize that you don't know for sure if you will get to be with your family in heaven, so you need to make the most of the life that you have with them right now. Strive to strengthen your relationship with your family.

56: Give birth to your daughter and have your life be changed forever, in ways that you could never even imagine. Watch your dad burst into tears when he gets to hold his granddaughter for the first time. Get the impression that this is what heaven is supposed to feel like: joy and love, instead of frustration and confusion. Gain the conviction that you want to feel more of this in your life.

57: Three weeks after giving birth, have the government shut down all non-essential businesses due to the outbreak of Covid-19. Learn that church meetings are cancelled because of it. Feel relief that you won't have to go back to church with your newborn just yet. Realize that your weeks feel calmer when you aren't going to church than the weeks when you are.

58: Watch your husband bless your child as a child of

record in the church. Record the blessing, even though recording prayers is frowned upon. Keep this recording to share with your daughter when she gets older.

59: Argue with your husband about your role as a mother. Tell him you envisioned yourself continuing with going to college while he tells you he anticipated you would quit to be a stay-at-home mom. Continue to take online classes during the pandemic.

60: Finish your associate's degree. Argue with your husband about the use of daycare so that you can get your bachelor's degree. Decide to put your daughter in the university's daycare and keep going to college. Learn about critical thinking and apply it to what you learn in church. Learn about sexual assault for the first time and finally feel relief about what you did in high school. Tell your husband that you think you were sexually assaulted in high school and have him give you a confused look and ask, "Are you sure?"

61: Go back to attending church after the pandemic. Grow to despise callings because you are forced to do a job for free, that you ought to be paid for, all because the church that owns billions of dollars wants to save money and tells you that you will be blessed for serving god by doing your calling.

62: Have your ministering sister invite you to a girls night. Show up at her house and participate in scripture and testimony sharing. Feel like she lied to you about actually having a girls night so that she could cross her ministering duties off of her list. Grow to despise ministering because it feels like you are forced into making a fake, disingenuous friendship.

63: Grow to loathe the differences between how men and women are treated in the church. Despise that the church controls every aspect of your life from what you wear, to how you parent, and realize that you don't want your daughter to be treated poorly because she was born into the church as a female.

64: Read the family proclamation and have a spiritual revelation that gender is divinely appointed by god but sex is not, and that's why the LGBTQ community exists. Tell your husband about your spiritual revelation and have him tell you that it's not right and not of God. Wonder why you felt like you were given a spiritual revelation if it's not really "from god," and ponder the meaning behind it.

65: Go to the temple with your spouse to participate in sealings for the dead. Think of the LGBTQ community

and how they are told that if they want to be in heaven
for eternity then they can't be with the person they truly
love. Feel confused, because that doesn't sound like what
a loving god would say, and living without your family
in heaven wouldn't feel like heaven at all. Get angry that
your LGBTQ friends can't have eternal marriage in the
temple like your cisgender, heterosexual friends.
Question your sexuality because of how angry you feel.

66: Watch your friends, family, and mission
buddies/acquaintances leave the church for various
reasons. Silently applaud them for having the courage to
leave and wish that you could do the same. Be surprised
that you feel this way and wonder if you actually ever
would leave.

67: Read Educated with your sister who served a mission
and marvel at everything that Tara Westover
experienced. Discuss how hard it is to keep believing in
the church sometimes. Realize that you are struggling
with your beliefs but be afraid to tell your husband for
fear that he will want to leave you. Continue to struggle
with your beliefs in silence and keep up the appearance
of being a firm, believing member.

68: Start reading other books about problematic church
history. Realize that sexism and racism has been the

foundation of the religion from the beginning. Realized
that you're not surprised by anything you're learning,
given that the church still struggles today with racism
and sexism.

69: Give a talk in sacrament meeting and instead of
sharing your testimony, rant about how you don't even
think the church is true because they are sexist, racist,
hate LGBTQ people, and promise blessings that don't
even come true. Then remember that you are supposed
to be giving a testimony and try to make things
spiritually-related at the end. Have the congregation
thank you for your "raw testimony" after your talk.

70: Have your husband ask you if you are okay after
church, because of how your "testimony" went. Confess
that you are struggling and that you might not believe in
anything anymore, and have him walk away in silence
instead of responding.

71: Attend an endowment ceremony in the temple.
Notice that the ceremony is shorter than it used to be
and they no longer ask women to veil their faces during
the prayer. Be put off by this and wonder why is was
ever mandated in the first place if it's not anymore. Also
feel hopeful that this is a sign the church is becoming
more progressive. Hope that someday they will change

the sealing ceremony to include LGBTQ marriages.

72: Graduate from college, buy a house, start working on baby #2, and move to a new neighborhood and church ward. When meeting the neighbors, feel annoyed every time someone asks if you are "members," as if there is only one organization you can be a member of, knowing full well that they are referencing the lds church.

73: Attend the new church ward. Feel cold and depressed everytime you walk into the building. Try going to relief society and leave after the speaker talks about their relative that "suffers from homosexuality," as if it's an illness. Request to not minister anymore and say no when you are offered your next calling.

74: Struggle with getting pregnant. When you don't have success, tell your husband that you want to get a tattoo, and have him respond that, "You can do what you want, but just know tattoos aren't sexy."

75: Tell your husband a couple months later that you are getting a tattoo because he said you could, and it would help take your mind off not being pregnant. Then have him give you the silent treatment for a week. Try to ask his opinion on designs and placements and have him respond coldly each time.

76: The day before your tattoo appointment, remind your husband that you are getting a tattoo and have him respond, "I will try really hard to not think of you differently." Spend two hours locked in the bathroom crying. Reconcile with your husband and get your tattoo. Have him inspect the tattoo after your appointment and hear him say, "It looks simple enough that you could easily get it removed if you regret it later."

77: Continue trying to get pregnant with no success. Experience the loss of pregnancy through your niece's stillbirth. Feel guilt about continuing to try to get pregnant, after your sister-in-law lost a baby, and stop trying.

78: Keep going to church, but be open to your husband about the things you don't like. Bring up difficult topics of discussion with him and have him respond each time by saying, "That's something we will ask Jesus in Heaven" Feel frustrated by the continuous ending of conversations. Stop praying, because you don't want to pray to a misogynistic god anymore.

79: Three months later, have your husband confess that he isn't sure if he wants to be married to you anymore because your religious beliefs have changed and the

reason why he wanted to marry you was because you
were strong in the church. Feel your world immediately
flip upside down, crash, and burn.

80: Spend six months going to individual and couples'
therapy to try and work things out. Come out of each
therapy session feeling more hopeless than the time
before, while your husband comes out feeling more
hopeful. Be angry that you two come out feeling such
opposite things. Start to see the lack of compatibility
between you and your spouse.

81: Be asked by a bishopric member to pray in sacrament
meeting. See this as a potential sign from God that he
wants you to be a part of the church. Accept the
assignment and ponder about what you are going to say
in your prayer. The day that you are supposed to pray in
sacrament meeting, receive a text from a different
bishopric member, saying that he has asked someone
else to pray because you lack the testimony needed to
pray in sacrament meeting. Read in the text that he will
be happy to have you pray once you regain your
testimony. Feel as if he verbally slapped you in the face,
and feel as if God doesn't actually want you.

82: Feel hopeless, alone, and not accepted for your
beliefs. Start listening to the Mormon Stories podcast to

feel less alone. Realize others feel the same way as you and that you're not crazy for feeling how you feel. Realize that you matter and your life path matters. Realize that you want your daughter to have a full, happy life and that you want to raise her to have a strong, independent personality. Fear what will happen to her and her self image if she becomes a teenager in the church.

83: Realize that if you never became a mother, you might have never seen the things that bother you about the church. Realize that caring for a tiny human has made you more aware of how the church influences others, that it wasn't so bad when it was just influencing you, but realizing it could influence your children negatively changed how you view everything. Realize that without your daughter, you may have never had the courage to leave the church. Decide to get a divorce to give you and your daughter a reset to your life.

84: Move out of the home you lived in for only eight months. Stop going to church entirely. Start trying things like alcohol, and coffee to try and break free from the lds lifestyle. Stop wearing garments, start wearing tank tops. Try to have a more positive view of yourself as an imperfect individual.

85: Attend church with your sister to watch her son get blessed. Record the blessing for her because you know she would definitely appreciate it, even if it's traditionally frowned upon. After the blessing, share your testimony about how you prayed to know, and got the answer no, And that getting a "no" is just as valid as getting a "yes." Do this with the hope that, if someone like you feels alone, they can now know that they aren't alone. Leave the church, lose all your mormon friends, upset your mormon family members, and hope for the best for your future.